Forex Trading

30 Highly Effective Tips and Tricks to Start Properly, Avoid Major Mistakes, and Maximize Your Profits with Forex Trading

Anthony Kreil

liable for any hardship or damages that may befall them after undertaking information described herein.

Additionally, the information in the following pages is intended only for informational purposes and should thus be thought of as universal. As befitting its nature, it is presented without assurance regarding its prolonged validity or interim quality. Trademarks that are mentioned are done without written consent and can in no way be considered an endorsement from the trademark holder.

DISCLAIMER

Although the author and publisher have made every effort to ensure that the information in this book was correct at press time, the author and publisher do not assume and hereby disclaim any liability to any party for any loss, damage, or disruption caused by errors or omissions, whether such errors or omissions result from negligence, accident, or any other cause.

Table of Contents

Introduction

Congratulations on downloading *Forex Trading:30 Highly Effective Tips and Tricks to Start Properly, Avoid Major Mistakes, and Maximize Your Profits with Forex Trading* and thank you for doing so. While successfully trading in the forex market can be extremely complicated, that doesn't mean there aren't a number of vital tips that can help jumpstart you through the early, awkward, learning portion of the process as quickly as possible.

To that end, the following chapters will discuss 30 of the most effective tips and tricks when it comes to trading in the forex market successfully, broken up into three categories. The first includes tips for what qualifies as the ideal forex trading mindset as well as what you can do to develop it for yourself. The second includes tips for the act of trading itself and how to help maximize your overall successful trade percentage with every trade you make. Finally, the third includes tips to help ensure you earn big money while working for it as little as possible. From there you will then find a few quick success stories of successful forex traders, told in their own words, to help give you hope on the days when your successful trade percentage is at its lowest.

There are plenty of books on this subject on the market, thanks again for choosing this one! Every effort was made to ensure it is full of as much useful information as possible, please enjoy!

Chapter 1:
Mindset Tips

Keep a close watch on your mindset: If you ever hope to find more than a base level of success in the forex market then there are any number of things you will need to learn and skills you will want to master. One of the first of these skills that you are going to want to hone is the ability to maintain a forex trading mindset over a prolonged period of time. Specifically, what this means is that you are going to need to learn to keep a cool head regardless of the situation that you find yourself presented with. Your goal should ultimately get to a point where you don't let in any emotions at all while trading to ensure that nothing interferes with your established trading plan.

Remember, the only thing that you should really are about while trading is the numbers as anything else is just going to get in the way. Being successful in the forex market frequently requires making important decisions on the fly and the only way of ensuring that you are making the right choices is if you are certain that emotion doesn't enter into the equation. While the idea here is pretty straightforward, it can be harder than you might expect to implement which is why you will likely find that you have better success when you focus on removing one emotion from the equation as a time.

Don't let yourself get angry: Anger can be a complex emotion to deal with while trading as it is possible for it to be affecting your judgement a great deal while at the same time assuming that you are trading in a perfectly rash and reasonable matter. As such, when it comes to getting rid of your anger once and for all the first thing you will need to do is to focus on establishing an emotional/mental baseline that you stick to when trading so that you have an easy way to determine when you are straying from the mark.

While it is perfectly natural to feel angry when a trade that seemed like a sure thing suddenly turned around at the last second, if you give into that anger for more than the second in which it flares up, you are going to start losing track of what you are trying to accomplish in favor of angry and useless pursuits such as vengeance on a market that has already moved on to the next big thing. As such, rather than letting your anger influence your trading process, focus on learning to respond to unexpected issues more quickly as a means of minimizing unexpected losses while at the same time feeling good about doing so.

Focus on yourself: If you are looking for a way to lose money in the forex market, there will never be a more effective means of doing so than by trying to follow the trading plans that work for other people. A trading plan is an extremely personal expression of your goals for the forex market and the way that you are going to interact with it. As such, it requires plenty of trial and error, as well as personal introspection to ensure that it works with your natural trading tendencies as opposed to against them.

While looking at the level of success that professional traders have can make it difficult to forge your own path, mimicking what they are trying to do is only going to ultimately prove to be an exercise in futility. It is important to instead avoid the temptation by keeping in mind that knowing yourself and your strengths and weaknesses are the most reliable path to success.

Know your acceptable level of risk going in: Having a clear idea of what level of risk is acceptable to you, before you ever make your first trade is a must for a few key reasons. First, it will save you the trouble of having to determine such a thing at the moment, when every second could be literally costing you money while also making it difficult to think about anything else. Determining your level of risk aversion is as easy as considering if you prefer slow and steady profits from your trades or investments or if you are comfortable with the idea of a greater degree of risk in exchange for the potential of a much greater reward over all.

Additionally, it will make it much easier for you to choose appropriate strategies and trading styles to adopt because you will be able to automatically cut out a large portion of the available options. Understanding your personal style will make it easier for you to find time tables and strategies that play to your strengths and mitigate your weaknesses rather than choosing those that force you to struggle against your natural inclinations. Failing to take such things into account might work in the short-term, but in the long run, it is only going to cause you additional grief.

Understand what you are up against: While it can be easy to look at overnight success stories of traders who hit it big early in their trading careers and assume that the forex market is a road to easy riches, the reality is actually far more complicated than that which is why it is so important to be realistic when it comes to your expectations regarding your results and to trade accordingly. While leverage makes such things technically possible if you jump right into leverage trading the only thing you are going to do is find a way to force yourself into the type of hole that it will be quite difficult to get out of moving forward.

This means that grounding your expectations when going in is an effective way to ensure that you can focus on making money on a consistent basis first, before trying to reach the big leagues. As an added bonus, this realistic approach will help to ensure you don't make the mistake of overtrading or overleveraging your position in an effort to pull success from the jaws of defeat at the last moment. While such moves could generate big positive swings in the short-term, they are almost never going to hold up much longer than that.

Don't give in to fear: Besides anger, the most commonly felt emotion while trading is fear. Fear is particularly devious as it can skew your perspective in such a way that it is difficult to do anything but watch as a previously solid trade crumbles for no discernible reason. Like anger, it is natural to be a little fearful when it comes to making big trades, especially those of the high risk, high reward variety. Additionally, if you are heavily invested in a specific currency to the point where you perhaps used funds that had other uses, then watching the progress of a given trade once it has been made is always sure to be a little nerve wracking.

While being angry can easily cloud your judgement, being afraid can leave you feeling paralyzed, unable to make the types of split-second decisions that can reverse a major loss and turn it to little more than a simple bump in the road. There are two big ways to get over your fears, the first of which is by carefully considering the trades you do make so that you can remain confident throughout and the second is to practice,

practice, practice as the more you do so the more the more comfortable the entire process will feel.

Never take anything personally: When it comes to trading it is important to keep in mind that you are not a beautiful and unique snowflake and that the market doesn't care about you one way or another. As such, it is impossible for the market to do anything to personally mess you up which means you can't take the things that happen to you personally as doing so will only lead to unproductive behave in the long run. It can be easy for new traders to grow too attached to a given trade, purely based on emotional reasons. In your mind, every trade that you make should only matter to you in a purely financial sense, thinking about it in any other terms is a surefire way to start making mistakes and end up mismanaging your trading account in a big way.

Additionally, it is important to always remember that making a number of unlikely trades in a row doesn't make you a fantastic trader, just as not making a successful trade for a day, or even a week doesn't make you a bad trader. Remaining neutral is the only reliable way to ensure your emotions don't come into play and end up skewing your numbers and causing a greater degree of loss than you might expect.

Compartmentalize everything: If you ever hope to trade successfully in the long tern it is important to learn to compartmentalize each trade which means not letting any single trade, regardless of how positive or negative it might be, affect your overall trading outlook. Regardless if you are reacting to something negative or something positive, letting any thought in that is not about the trade you are currently focused on is a surefire way to kiss all of your potential profits goodbye.

In order to counter this common mistake you are going to want to strive to avoid becoming too confident, and also avoid making trades because you are trying to make up for a previously disastrous trade. If you ever find yourself losing objectivity in the moment, the best way to fix the problem is to simply stop trading for a time in an effort to clear your head and put some mental distance between you and whatever it is you are trying to get over. If you find your previous trades hanging over your head regularly then you are sure to end up splitting your focus rather than putting it all where it needs to be, solely on the trade that you are going to be making to ensure that you continue to manage your money correctly.

Understand every trade is a tool: May new forex traders make the mistake of personifying specific trades they hold on to for purely emotional reasons this is only going to ultimately cause you trouble in the long run, however, as it is important that you keep in mind the fact that you could have to jettison the most effective trade of your life on a moment's notice if the market says its time has come.

Using every trade to its fullest also means understanding that even when a trade doesn't go according to plan, it is still performing a very useful function by filling out the statistical average on your plan to ensure that you are more likely to make a successful trade next time. For example, assuming you create a trading plan with a 60 percent success rate, then you still need to expect to lose out on 40 percent of your trades which means that even the losing trades fulfil a crucial function.

Learn to be patient: When it comes to dealing with the forex market in the long-term successfully patience and success go hand in hand. While early on it can be easy to feel as though the time you spend not trading is only time spent wasted, the fact of the matter is there are frequently going to be periods of time where the absolute best way to ensure your profits remain at a reasonable point will be to avoid trading in any way shape or form. The market moves in a wide variety of different ways, after all, and relatively few of them are going to result in the types of strong trends that you are looking for.

If you still feel the need to be constantly trading then you may want to consider the fact that a 7 percent return on investment is average and you can expect anywhere between five and 10 percent each month while trading in the forex market which means you will still be ahead of the game a majority of the time. As such, it makes more sense to worry instead about maximizing the trades you do make as opposed to making as many different trades as humanly possible.

Don't underestimate boredom: When you are in the midst of a major trade with a significant chunk of change on the line then trading in the forex market can be one of the most exciting things in the world. In reality, however, that is only about five percent of the overall experience, with the rest of it actually being fairly route and rather straightforward. What this means for your trading percentage is that if you don't take into account what boredom can do to your resolve then it could easily lead to an increase in mistakes that stem from a burning desire to do something, anything, regardless of the results just to end the boredom.

Needless to say, boredom is an extremely dangerous emotion and will lead to nothing but poor trading decisions if not kept in check. Luckily, as you make an active effort to cut down on inessential trading time you should find that you are naturally spending less time staring at a screen, so the problem should solve itself.

Chapter 2:
Trading Tips

Trade with a clear goal in mind: Regardless of where your overall skill level is out, ensuring that you only commit to a trade with a clear goal in mind will help to improve your successful trade percentage almost overnight. Trading without a clear set of goals is a surefire way to lose money, even if you are following a safe currency pair. In order to accurately determine what your goals should be, the first thing you will need to do is determine the amount of time you will want to spend trading each day and then stick with it. The amount of time you choose is important which means if something changes in your schedule you will want to rearrange things post haste.

You will also need to consider the amount of capital that you have on hand, in addition to the amount of risk you feel as though you can handle realistically. If you are typically a risk adverse individual then you will want to make fewer trades overall, as the trades you will make are going to be far more likely to succeed. On the contrary, if you have already decided that you appreciate a bit of risk in your life then making a greater number of riskier trades is going to be the way to go instead.

Consider market sentiment: If, despite your best efforts to determine the true market value of a particular currency or currency pair, things just don't seem to be lining up, then the reason for the discrepancy often lies in the fact that you did not accurately take into account market sentiment. If it is left unchecked, market sentiment is easily capable of altering the price of a given currency to a significant degree, simply because the way that other investors are thinking about a given currency is based largely around gut feelings and less about the facts of what the market is actually doing.

To ensure that you aren't going to have to deal with market sentiment drinking your milkshake, it is crucial that you expand your sites beyond the short-term charts to focus more on the big picture. Looking at only half the situation is a great way to make the mistake of assuming that an offshoot of a major trend is actually a trend in its own right. This will become easier as you become more familiar with the pairs you are working with as you will be able to tell if something is off about their regular movement at a glance. Until this happens, however, it is important to take things slow and to pay as close of attention to the market as possible.

Always check the relative level of risk: While occasionally you will come across trades that virtually scream they are going to be a sure thing, acting on a hunch is always going to be the first step towards making a losing trade which is why it is so important to always do your homework to ensure a trade isn't going to end in disaster. In fact, before you go ahead and purchase any currency pair it is crucial that you look at it from every angle which means learning not just how likely it is that you will make a profit, but also the odds that you will lose everything on the trade instead. This is why it is so important to use technical analysis, fundamental analysis, or both as if you can't determine the way the wind is blowing in the market then you will have no way to know if you are following a trend or setting one.

Set clear boundaries for every trade: In order to ensure that you can get the most out of any given trade it is important to determine a point where you are going to cut your losses and try again another time. You will also want to have a firm point in mind where you will be satisfied with your profits and can get out of the current trade, happy with the amount of profit you made. Once you have both of these points firmly determined, you will then be able to see just what the breadth of the risk that the given trade is saddling you with as well as the greatest amount of payout you can expect assuming things go your way.

After you take the time to line everything up in this way then you will want to see that the odds of success are greater than the odds of failure by 2 to 1, though 3 to 1 is better, then you are better off trying something else, or changing some of the variables associated with the trade as it is not in your best interest to proceed forward as is.

Never stay in past your exit point: Assuming you go ahead with the trade in the above tip, and further assuming that the trade goes according to plan, you will then need to ensure that you never stay in the trade past the point you determined as your exit point as this will skew the numbers involved in the trade, possibly turning a good choice into a bad choice in the process. What's more, generally speaking, you are never going to make more by staying in and trying to earn the last few cents on a trade then you have the potential for losing assuming things suddenly, and violently turn against you.

If you do end up chasing a trend that is extremely strong, then when you get to the predetermined exit point you have another option as well. Instead of selling off all of your holdings you can instead only sell off half of what you have invested so far, before choosing another exit point for the remaining half that takes into account the strength of the new trend. This way you protect some of your profits while at the same time taking advantage of the better than average trend you have found.

Don't forget liquidity: If you hope to eliminate as much risk as possible from each of your trades, you are always going to need to consider the current liquidity levels that line up with your chosen currency pairs, otherwise you may find that there is not enough movement expected to actually make things worth your while. In fact, the importance of liquidity directly increases the less trading capital you have available to you, making it especially useful for new forex traders.

What this means is that when you are first starting out you are going to want to a make a point of never invest more than 2 percent of your total available trade capital in a signal trade.

This means that if you star off with $5,000 to trade with then you are never going to want to use more than $100 to invest in a single trade for a currency pair. While this limit is sure to chafe when you are on a roll, it will actually serve to help protect you from mistakes in both the short and the long-term. Think of it this way, it ensures that you have to make 50 bad trades in a row in order to deplete your trading capital entirely, something that is difficult for even the greenest traders to manage.

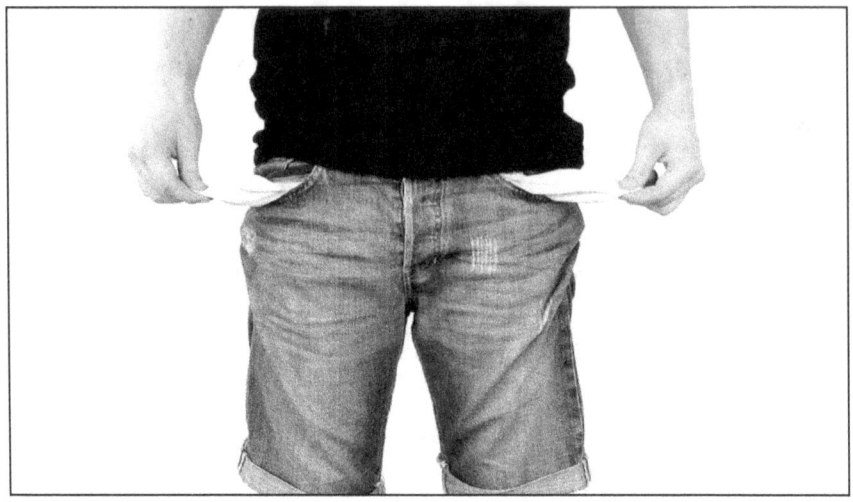

Never trade what you can't afford to lose: In order to ensure that you are going to be able to trade successfully with the trading capital you do have available, one of the first things you are going to want to do is determine how much you can realistically afford to lose. This isn't a question you should take lightly either, picture a pile of bills on the floor and visualize them going up in smoke. Whatever amount you can do so with and not immediately feel anxious is the amount you should start trading with.

While this might seem like a silly exercise, the fact of the matter is that trading with money you can't afford to lose which splits your focus and causes you to be more likely to lose the funds than would otherwise be the case. If you try and trade with money that you should be spending on living expenses instead, then you are going to be much more cautious when making trades which will eventually lead you to missing out on trades that you should have profited from if you weren't so worried about maintaining your trade balance.

Always test new strategies cautiously: Whenever you come across a new strategy that you are anxious to try, it is important to always do so in a low-stakes but live environment rather than with a test trading account. The reasoning for this is that as long as there is real money on the line you can be reasonably sure you are responding in the way you would when it counts, something you can't expect when you know that everything you are doing is fake.

Assuming the early tests are promising, you will then want to up the ante but continue testing for at least another week until you are sure you know exactly what adopting it is going to do for your successful trade percentage. Only by constantly hitting an acceptable trade percentage will you be able to confidently know that the strategies you are using are the right ones for your personal trading plan. Don't forget, just because you have come across a few that really work for you is no reason to stop exploring the wide variety of options that are available to you out there, you never know when you might stumble across your new favorite.

Cut down on your micromanaging: While certain trades are always going to require a more hands on approach, many new traders spend far too much time watching their trades move pip by pip which gives them plenty of time to start second guessing themselves by moving stop losses that don't need to be moved or by searching for additional confirmation for a trade that was already clearly moving in a given direction. Tasks like these add nothing productive to the process and only increase the likelihood that mistakes are going to be made at some step in the process.

What's more, this type of superfluous activity tends to bring about changes to your trading plan as well. As changes made in the heat of the moment are never going to be as reliable as the plan that you came up with when you were at your most clear-headed. This is not to say that you will never need to improvise, but there is certainly a time and a place for that sort of thing and it certainly isn't in the middle of a trade that's already going about as well as can be expected. Trading successfully is all about being able to stick to a plan in a way that is reliable enough to be counted on no matter what, the fact that it also means you don't have to spend countless hours micromanaging each and every trade is just an added bonus.

Understand the differences in margin: When it comes to trading in the forex market it is important to keep in mind that margin works differently in this instance than it does elsewhere. What this means is that when trading in the forex market you will want to cease thinking of equity as a type of down payment on equity for the future. Instead, you will need to think of it as a sort of account deposit that can be useful to have when it comes to things like mitigating losses related to recent trades or those that may yet materialize at a future point and time. Generally speaking, the greater the options for leverage from your dealer or broker, the higher the margin for the trade is likely to be.

Furthermore, when it comes to the forex market, it is important to keep in mind that yield and return are directly connected with one another. What this essentially means is that every time you complete a forex trade the currency you sell is paying for the currency you buy. This doesn't mean you will no longer need to account for interest, however, as you will pay it on the currencies you sell while earning it on the currencies you buy.

Chapter 3:
Tips for Trading Less Without Sacrificing Profits

*C*ut out unnecessary trades: When they are first getting started in the forex market, many trades end up making plenty of trades that ultimately don't end up doing much of anything and, at best, end up paying for their own dealer or broker fees. While these sorts of trades are certainly much preferred to those that end up actually costing you money, you will want to make a point of avoiding them as much as possible in the long run.

You see, in addition to costing you in fees here and there, these sorts of trades are draining your mental resources, if not necessarily your physical ones. If you are spending too much of your time focusing on trades that ultimately go nowhere, eventually you are going to be unable to give the required time to a trade that would have actually worked out for you in the end. If you find yourself falling into this trap, the easiest way to get out of it is to simply start selecting trades with a higher potential for profit. While you will encounter additional risk, you will be sure that your potential for reward is great enough to make the whole process worthwhile overall.

Watch the spread: In addition to taking hits from over trading, one of the best ways to increase your profit per trade is to ensure you are properly taking into account the bid-ask spread for each of your trades. While it may take a little extra time in order to ensure you have all the relevant information, doing so can change the amount you end up paying or end up earning dramatically and the importance of doing so cannot be overstated.

As there are very few limitations when it comes to the forex market, the spread you might find in some scenarios could be dramatically skewed against you, which it can be helpful to know if you want to ensure you are always maximizing your profits. Even if you don't find yourself spending too much per trade on the surface, you could still easily spend about five percent of the cost of a trade on the spread if you aren't careful, which is nothing to sneeze at.

Use rollovers to your advantage: While it won't happen to everyone, there are some people who will be good, and lucky, enough at trading in the forex market that they have to pay taxes on their profits in order to stay on the good side of the IRS. Of those, a smaller few will find that their earnings have actually pushed them into a higher tax bracket, significantly decreasing their overall profits in the long-term. If you end up having a good year then it is very important to know the laws regarding tax brackets in your area as there is often more you can do than just except your fate.

A good example of this is when it is near the end of the year and you have a few trades that you need to complete. While most forex trades have 48 hours to be completed, if you initiate a rollover you can have an additional two days to complete your business in exchange for paying a small premium. This can be done indefinitely which means you can easily move profits between quarters, or even between fiscal years if it is in your best interests to do so.

Don't forget about slow turnover: While heavy turnover certainly has the potential to take its toll on your portfolio if you aren't careful, the fact of the matter is that not having any lower turnover interests can also degrade the overall potential of your portfolio by denying it valuable components that can't be found elsewhere. Trying to follow every up-and-down tick of your favorite currency pairs, plus all the news headlines that could affect them, can leave many investors feeling a little strung out. As a consequence of this, they often end up becoming more erratic in their trading habits before ultimately resulting in making crucial choices on little more than impulse and pure adrenaline.

Regardless of the type of trader you are, it is important to balance out your trading style, and if you tend to favor one over the other, ween yourself off this approach as time goes on. In fact, if you do end up successfully lowering your turnover rate, and instead spend that time doing more research, then the odds are good you will find that the trades you ultimately do end up making are going to uniformly be more successful than would otherwise be the case. As a general rule, one of the most commonly missed opportunities when it comes to ensuring the success of a high turnover portfolio comes from the mistaking of not taking advantage of any of the guaranteed payments that come along with reliable payments on interest such as what you would see from a carry trade.

Diversification is key: Regardless of your reasons for getting into the forex market in the first place, you can virtually guarantee that there is a better choice out there for you than simply trying a little bit of everything and seeing what sticks. If you do prefer your trading be as hands on as possible, one good choice is to consider diversifying the currency pairs that you regularly hold as this will give you something productive to do with your excess trading energy besides fiddling with a single currency pair trade that doesn't really need any extra work.

As an added bonus, once you have diversified properly you won't ever have to worry about a single bad swing of the market wiping out all of your holdings in a single stroke of bad luck. Even if you find that you still appear to be making the same number of trades overall, the amount of reward you get for your effort is likely to be far higher as the effort you put in will all be rewarded with real results. As you will be making fewer trades you will also be making fewer mistakes as well.

Hire a professional: One surefire way to ensure that you have to spend less time trading each week, while still holding onto your profits, is to hire a professional to do the work for you. While this might not seem feasible at first, the fact of the matter is that it is more manageable than it might first seem. First, while the costs will mean you will have to accept a somewhat smaller profit margin, the difference will be offset by the fact that the professional is likely to generate more profits, more regularly than what you can manage yourself. When you add to this the additional profits you can make with the time you now have available as you aren't spending it trading you may even come out ahead.

What's more, you likely aren't giving up total control of your account, unless you want to, as you will still be able to tell them the type of strategies you prefer to follow as well as what your long-term and short-term goals might be. Unfortunately, a quality forex investment service doesn't come cheap and you will likely need to have around $50,000 on hand to ensure that you qualify for most privately managed forex accounts.

Don't discount the long-term: While a short-term forex approach is definitely going to be the right choice in any number of trading scenarios, if you aren't planning on actively capitalizing on your profits at the moment, then long-term choices might be a better fit. Not only will they ensure that you have to do less work at the moment, it can actually ensure that your profit margin greatly extends along with the extended timeline.

Essentially, when you reinvest your early profits back into the market, you stand to make quite a bit more in the long-term, especially if you are planning on letting your earnings grow to maximize multiple decades of potential growth. This is why it is crucial to reinvest often and early to maximize your profits in both the long and the short-term. This process is known as compounding and if you are a new investor with more than 20 years left before retirement then it is likely the single most powerful tool in your arsenal.

To understand why this is the case, take a look at the average 25-year-old. If their goal is to make $1,000,000 through investment by the time they retire (35 years in the future) they would want to save an average of $880 per month, assuming they were able to see a slightly below average return of 5 percent each year. On the contrary, if they waited until they were 45 to start investing then they would need to save $3,200 per month if they still hoped to retire at age 60.

Cast a wider net: An alternative to the near constant stream of research you likely find yourself doing as a new forex trader is to instead keep an eye out for the currency pairs that are going to be the most tradable each day based on their viewable statistics. If you then cast an even wider net and watch for potential options to pop you will then be in a position where you can more easily maximize your profits through the trade as quickly and effectively as possible. Even better, you also cut out the directional bias as you will then be able to move in multiple directions based on the state of the market when everything is said and done.

In order to decrease your workload even more, you could also choose to work from a wider timeframe so that the amount of research you have to do decreases accordingly. Depending on the types of trades that you are interested in, you should be able to set the screen to look for small and consistent movement just as easily as large, slower options as well.

Don't forget the 80/20 rule: The 80/20 rule says that 80 percent of your trading results should come from just 20 percent of your actions. While this is snappy to say, most traders don't quite understand where they need to emphasize their time and where it should be cut short. As a general rule, you can expect better results if you spend more time doing things like reviewing your performance and creating guidelines based on it that match your trading strategy. You will also want to do things like creating a watchlist of currencies that may soon be viable, guarantee you have the right alerts set and always keep a journal of your failures and your successes.

This also means you are going to want to keep extremely detailed notes when it comes to the types of trades you make so that you can more easily learn your own personal patterns, some of which may not be visible in any other way. This means you are going to want to do more than simply track your failures and success but also how the final state of the trade was determined and what your emotional state was like the entire time. Once you have enough examples to see the patterns you will want to strengthen the positive ones through conscious usage and do your best to minimize the negatives.

Chapter 4:
Success Stories

*J*ay: Trading for me is supplemental, it is not full time. I trade swing trades (I take what the market produces and catch and ride the waves). I also trade price action.

I am a self-taught trader and for a long time stuck to a few systems I clicked with (I only ever really liked the Cowabunga), but I wanted to come up with my own system. After trying indicators that only tell you what happened I decided to trade PA. My System is pure money management and proper leverage. I trade with naked charts, I see the market better. Momentum based trading. Sometimes I will throw a volume indicator on there that is only if I am looking at a huge trend change. I do follow COT (Commitment of Traders) sometimes only to get a sense and confirmation of true direction.

After blowing a few accounts I started trading the PA. I average between 30 to hundreds of pips (It all depends on the market). I even snagged over 1K of pips in one single currency at one time. What got to me to lose the money I made was greed and over leveraging after I started kicking ass. I quickly was humbled. Opened a new account of $75 couple weeks ago, trading 2K lots is now approximately $110. Once I get to $500 I will go to trading 3K lots. Till I hit $1K.

Patience is a virtue and I will be a successful trader and I am over my losing barrier and currently approaching my barrier to success.

I took my one and only trade today selling EUR/AUD at 1.26258 @ 2K lot site (.20 a pip). account up by $5 today so far I plan on waking up to about $20 in profit with this current trade. that is a 10% increase on my account tomorrow if successful. I have already set my stop to lock in 2 pips and let the trade run. I am risk free at this point. The market will either give me the bias or I will be stopped out and the joke is on my broker... Yes, I like to make my broker eat the spread. This is also part of my strategy.

Marc: I trade full time from home for a living. I've been doing this for four years now though I traded part time for several years before that.

I trade just the EUR/USD market strictly on a day trading basis, looking to take 10-30 points out the market by following strong current momentum. I use a maximum 20 point stop - always there, no exceptions - and I'm quick to move the stop up to breakeven for a free trade, even if I do get scratched out many times.

Without taking large risks - I don't risk more than 1% of my account on any trade - I can now consistently make 40%-60% pa uncompounded return on capital. So, if you wanted to make $50,000 pa you'd need comfortably over $100,000 to make this viable. Preferably you want quite a lot more in reserve as you always want the ability to recapitalize if you have a bad run or do something really rash.

The biggest issue is not your method - it doesn't have to be great, it just needs to have a positive edge - it's the discipline, strict risk control and emotional stability required just to grind it out day after day without taking any big hits. Getting to this state of mind and consistent behavior took me many years, much frustration, and a lot of losses.

It's not easy, it takes time and experience, and you do require a material capital sum. But it can be done if you really, really, want it and take it seriously like a career, not a bit of part time entertainment.

Conclusion

Thank you for making it through to the end of *Forex Trading: 30 Highly Effective Tips and Tricks to Start Properly, Avoid Major Mistakes, and Maximize Your Profits with Forex Trading*, let's hope it was informative and able to provide you with all of the tools you need to achieve your goals, whatever it is that they may be. Just because you've finished this book doesn't mean there is nothing left to learn on the topic, expanding your horizons is the only way to find the mastery you seek. Furthermore, if you ever hope to truly find success you are going to need to ensure that this is not a one off thing, rather you need to become a lifelong learner who is never content to rest on their laurels and who is always anxious to learn a new strategy or type of analysis that will surely put them head and shoulders above the competition.

While these tips are enough to ensure that your forex trading career is sure to be fruitful, there is still far more information to learn on the topic if you ever hope to be truly successful. Two good places to start include: *Forex Trading: How to Make Serious Money Trading Forex (Even if You're a Complete Beginner)* and *Forex Trading: Crash Course to Quickly Get Set Up and Make Instant Cash Trading Forex* to help ensure that you get a better overall feel for forex trading as a whole.

Finally, if you found this book useful in any way, a review on Amazon is always appreciated!

www.ingramcontent.com/pod-product-compliance
Lightning Source LLC
Chambersburg PA
CBHW071157220526
45468CB00003B/1057